NatureStructure
Infrastructure for Nature

By Scott Burnham

NATURESTRUCTURE.COM

Print Edition January 2020

ISBN: 978-1-945971-05-1

For all correspondence, contact Scott Burnham at sb@scottburnham.com

Cover Image: Living Seawalls by Reef Design Lab

ABOUT THE AUTHOR

Scott Burnham, FRSA, has created resourceful and resilient design initiatives in over a dozen cities worldwide and more than thirty exhibitions in eight countries.

He is the founder of Reprogramming the City, a global initiative to improve cities and the environment by repurposing and reimagining the function of existing urban assets.

Burnham has addressed The World Bank, The World Urban Development Congress, and many other organizations on resilient design strategies. He the author of *Reprogramming the City, Design Hacking, Trust Design, Urban Play*, and a contributor to publications ranging from The Guardian to Architizer.

In recognition of his work, Burnham was made a Fellow of the RSA (Royal Society for the encouragement of Arts, Manufactures and Commerce) in London in 2009.

For more information, visit scottburnham.com

TABLE OF CONTENTS

INTRODUCTION

> "Nature is already, in its forms and tendencies, describing its
> own design. Let us interrogate the great apparition, that shines
> so peacefully around us."
>
> *- Ralph Waldo Emerson*

The history of the built environment could be considered a battle against nature: barricading cities and coasts with sea walls, building over wetlands and green terrain, dividing migration routes with motorways. Tremendous effort has gone into the long war against the natural world.

Yet as sea levels rise and the severity of floods, droughts, and climate change increase—while species and habitats decrease—such efforts to conquer nature have proven to be futile at best and destructive acts of ego at worst.

NatureStructure represents an end to the battle against nature.

NatureStructure is infrastructure designed for nature; work created to nurture and repair ecosystems and habitats and integrate natural processes into the built environment. Instead of combating the natural world, NatureStructure embraces nature as a core element of the built environment. Norwegians have a phrase for it: "Spille på lag med naturen" - "To play on the same team as nature." The Dutch call it "Building with nature."

I created NatureStructure as a vehicle to focus attention on a new generation of nature-centric design—projects and systems to address the problems human development has created for itself.

The first exhibition of NatureStructure was launched at the Boston Society of Architects BSA Space Gallery. It introduced a range of ideas to US audiences for the first time: the Delfland Sand Engine (page 27), a feat of engineering that uses coastal tides to distribute sand along the coast of the Netherlands to reverse erosion and protect against sea level rise; Pop-Up, a revolutionary parking garage by Denmark's Third Nature that rises in the city scape as its base absorbs rainwater overflow(page 37); and 3D printed reefs and seawalls by Australia's Reef Design Lab (pages 5, 7) to repopulate Sydney Harbor sea life and counter the depletion of reefs in the world's oceans.

The Boston edition of NatureStructure was significant for the impact it had in the region as its ideas took root—literally. Discussions began about installing a Floating Ecosystem (page 11) in an area of the Charles River. BESE-Elements (page 29) panels brought in from the Netherlands for the exhibition found their way to Nantucket to help restore its seagrass beds, and more.

Following the exhibition I was invited to Seville, Spain, to address the Water, Landscape, and Citizens International Conference on the principles at the heart of NatureStructure. The enthusiastic response was gratifying but that isn't what stays with me today.

In Seville I encountered so many people from across the professional spectrum who were treating nature as the ultimate end-user of their designs. It was clear a paradigm shift in the relationship between nature and the built environment had arrived. It inspired me to create more channels for NatureStructure to expand its reach and influence. So here we are.

The collection of projects shown here, largely taken from the first NatureStructure exhibition, is a snapshot of what is taking place in a new reality-based relationship with natural forces.

My work and research continues, and each week new examples emerge to show how a new generation of infrastructure is facing a changing climate and damaged environment in nature-centric, synergistic, collaborative ways; integrating with the new realities we face, not ignoring them.

Scott Burnham

"As a species we have passed the point of just preventing further damage to marine habitats. We need to rapidly start developing and trialing ways to repair the damage already done."

- Reef Design Lab

Living Seawalls (Fish Apartments)
Reef Design Lab
Melbourne, Australia

The sleek exterior of Sydney's Opera House extends beneath the waterline, creating a smooth, inhospitable surface for sea life. The rest of the harbor isn't much kinder—more than 50 percent of its foreshore has been developed and modified from its original state with modified environments and surfaces that lack shelter and breeding areas for aquatic species.

Reef Design Lab's "Fish Apartment" Living Seawalls provide the harbor's native species a place to hide from predators, lay eggs, and re-establish their populations. The panels also allow numerous smaller species and crustaceans to live on the harbor's walls, providing food and replenishing its ecosystem.

"Seawall enhancement is an opportunity that is too often missed," says Reef Design Lab. "Increasing the complexity of seawalls with specifically designed units enhances the commercial and environmental value by improving recreational fishing opportunities and habitat biodiversity. Living sea wall structures can also help to disperse wave energy therefore minimizing reflective waves within marinas and coastal developments."

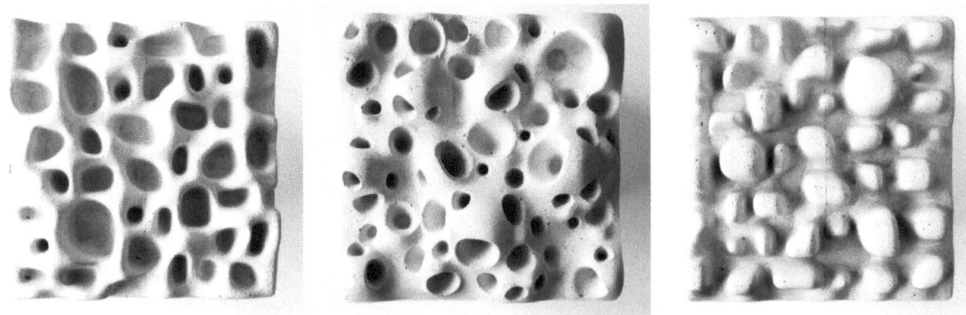

Honeycomb

Tide Pools

Swim Through

Ridges

Angles

Texture

Living Seawalls (Hex Panels)
Reef Design Lab and Sydney Institute of Marine Science
Sydney, Australia

Reef Design Lab has been working with Sydney Institute of Marine Science (SIMS) since 2015 to explore how 3D-printed geometry can be used to create habitat for native intertidal species to replenish the aquatic ecosystems of seawalls.

Different panel variations have been created to test which design works best to encourage native species colonization and foster biodiversity. The most effective design can then be incorporated into marine infrastructure on a larger scale.

100mm

530mm

550mm

The tiles have been designed to mimic the natural features of Sydney's rocky shores and are retrofitted to existing seawalls, with the expectation that they will remain there for at least 20 years.

The team is working toward a goal of "developing additional cost-effective habitat-enhancing structures, such as seawall blocks, that can be produced and installed during seawall construction or renovation."

Reef Design Lab, dedicated to "better design below the waterline," believes "man-made structures such as jetties, rock walls and marinas can include design features that create opportunities for nature rather than take them away and thus help maintain or even enhance biodiversity."

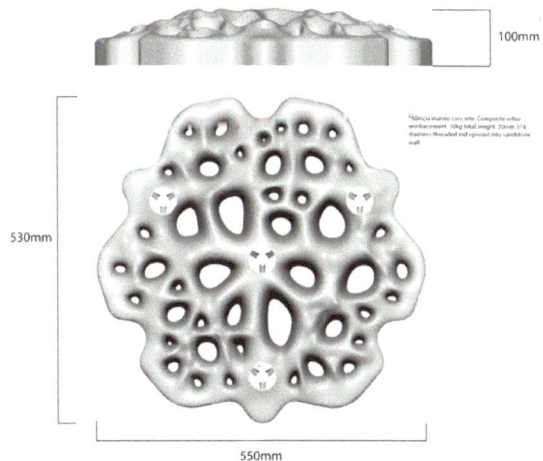

Singapore Sea Wall Tiles
Dr. Lynette H. L. Loke
Singapore

The island nation of Singapore has a strong relationship to the sea–one that has been far from mutually beneficial. As it has grown, the island has expanded on reclaimed land and surrounded itself with shear sea walls. Almost 80 percent of Singapore's coastal areas have hard sea walls or stone embankments.

"Together," notes Marine ecologist Peter Todd, "land reclamation and sea walls tend to result in the loss of entire habitats, as opposed to individual species."

Since 2009, Dr. Lynette H. L. Loke, a postdoctoral research fellow at the Experimental Marine Ecology Laboratory, National University of Singapore, has been developing a system to counter the damage Singapore has done to its seafront.

"There is a growing realization," says Loke, "that there is a need to look beyond the seawalls' negative impact and to find ways they can be built to improve their value as a habitat."

Loke has designed and installed more than 700 experimental concrete tiles onto the sea walls surrounding Singapore. Using custom software she developed, Loke measures the effectiveness of each tile design, then modifies it to maximize its effectiveness for habitat restoration, and to understand how habitat complexity affects the biodiversity of waterfront aquatic species.

Floating Ecosystems
Biomatrix Water
Forres, Scotland

Urban waterways that were once used as industrial passageways and dumping grounds are finally being recognized for their potential to improve the environment and public wellbeing.

Yet the history of these waterways have left scars. The gently sloping and shallow wetlands that once bordered city rivers have been replaced by steel and concrete embankments. The river banks have lost both their natural fauna and the ability to trap and filter pollutants to keep the water clean and sustain wildlife.

Biomatrix Water has developed "Floating Ecosystems" to restore the natural functions of lost urban riverbanks.

The structures grow plants on interlocking modular flotillas that act like floating water treatment plants and ecosystem support units, cleaning the water below and providing natural habitats and foraging sites for birds, bees, and smaller species.

"The native plants in our floating islands are selected for their benefits to local biodiversity, their intricate and deep-growing root systems, and their beauty," says Biomatrix's Managing Director Galen Fulford.

"The plant roots grow down into the water and develop beneficial aquatic biofilms, which cleanse the water through the breakdown, absorption, and metabolic transformation of nutrients and impurities."

"Revitalizing degraded urban waterways offers an incredible opportunity to increase habitat and natural green space in the city," continues Fulford, "and returns natural wetland edges to the urban waterscape."

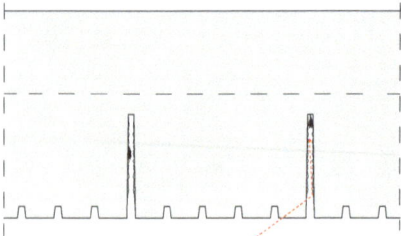

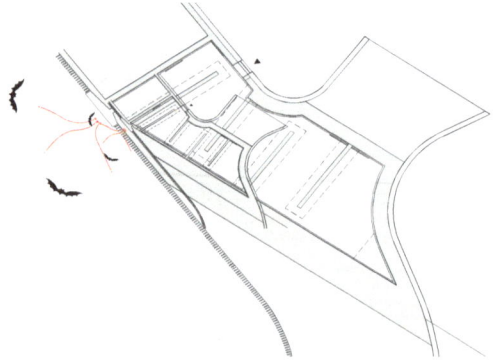

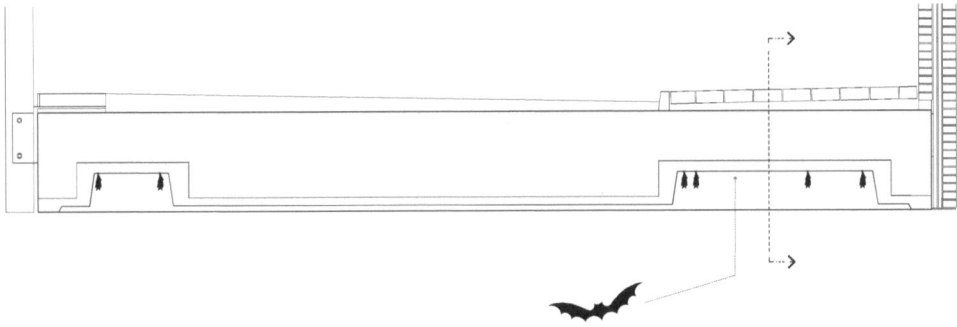

Vlotwateringbrug (Bat Bridge)
NEXT Architects
Monster, the Netherlands

Bats are a vital part of the ecosystem. They consume vast amounts of insects, including some of the most damaging agricultural pests, and pollinate many essential plants in the food chain.

Their utility in the ecosystem is drawing increased attention due to the fact that bat populations are in steep decline due to a variety of factors; a major one being loss of habitat and nesting areas as built environments expand.

The Vlotwateringbrug, often referred to as "the bat bridge," was designed for both local residents and the region's bat population. Located along the flight route of several bat species, NEXT Architects placed human needs and bat requirements on equal footing in the design process.

The thickness of its north side abutment provides winter shelter for bats, and its deck and brick balustrade house them during summer. The spacing between the wooden planks beneath the bridge was designed to a dimension wide enough let bats in, but narrow enough to keep predators out.

No bat-friendly detail was overlooked: the edges of the roosting areas were given a rough finish so the bats could grip its surface easily.

The bridge, says bat expert Marcel Schillemans from the Mammal Society, is "a textbook example of how a functional object can at the same time serve nature."

Tern Pontoons
Bureau Waardenburg
Markermeer, the Netherlands

"How do you deal with nature during a major dyke improvement?"

Not many infrastructure projects would spend much time on that question, but it was a central concern when construction began along the waterfront of Markermeer, the Netherlands—a major breeding area for the Common Tern.

Under the direction of the ecology and landscape consultancy Bureau Waardenburg, large pontoons "designed and developed based on the requirements of breeding Common Terns" were anchored 200 meters off the shoreline.

"The pontoons," says Bureau Waardenburg, "provide alternative breeding sites during a project to strengthen the dyke around lake and form an important part of the compensation measures."

Often referred to as "Tern Hotels," the pontoons were developed as an experiment under the "Marker Stepping Stone" project to strengthen links between the open water of Lake Marker and habitats inside the dyke.

In the first year the artificial breeding islands were home to 36 pairs of Common Terns, hatching 50 chicks. In the second year, numbers increased to more than 55 breeding pairs.

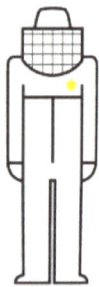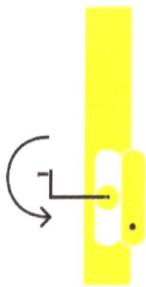

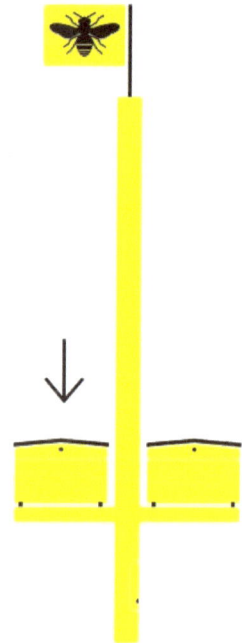

Sky Hive
Bee Collective
Maastricht, the Netherlands

Bees pollinate about 60 percent of our fruit and vegetables. Despite the vital role they play in our food supply, not much attention has been paid to their wellbeing as built environments expand.

Suburban growth, manicured lawns, homogeneous shrubbery, pesticides, and other factors have resulted in a rapidly declining bee population.

Research shows that bees do better in urban surroundings due to the variety of plants in parks and green pockets, so the Bee Collective set out to design a new system for supporting urban bee populations.

"Our answer to keeping bees in urban areas is the Sky Hive," says Bee Collective. "The Sky Hive is a pole with two beehives on it, which can be lifted up and down. When the hives are down, the beekeepers can take care of the bees."

"When the bees are back up on the pole, they are safe from vandalism. As the bees fly upwards when leaving the hives to collect pollen and nectar in a diameter of three kilometers from their home, there is no bigger chance to be stung by a bee under the pole than elsewhere."

Sky Hive also exists as a community education tool to increase appreciation of the role bees play in our ecosystem and food supply, and to train the next generation of beekeepers.

"By placing the Sky Hive in a public place, beekeeping is made accessible to all. Everybody interested can attend the meetings, observe the work of the beekeepers, or join in and take responsibility for the bees," says the group.

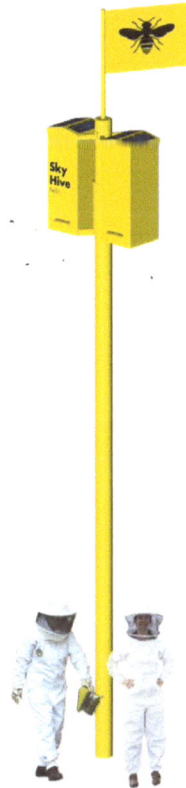

Batpole
Bee Collective
Maastricht, the Netherlands

"Quick! To the Batpole!"

When the rumblings of demolition or renovation disrupt the roosting areas of urban bats, this could be the call that goes out. Thanks to a team of designers in Maastricht, bats in the city will now have a place to go if their roosts are disrupted.

"The Batpole offers a temporary home for displaced bats and helps avoid delays in construction projects by offering alternate accommodation for this protected species," says the team. "At the same time, the Batpole points out the presence of bats in the urban biotope."

The designers behind the Batpole, Robin van Hontem, Daniel Meier and Janicke Kernland, are members of the Bee Collective, creators of the Sky Hive urban bee station.

They built upon their work on Sky Hive to provide a similar support station for urban bats. The Batpole rises seven meters into the air to provide disrupted bats with a safe home at a suitable height.

The team is working with ecologists to devise a way to lure bats to the Batpole before the sudden onset of construction drives them from their homes.

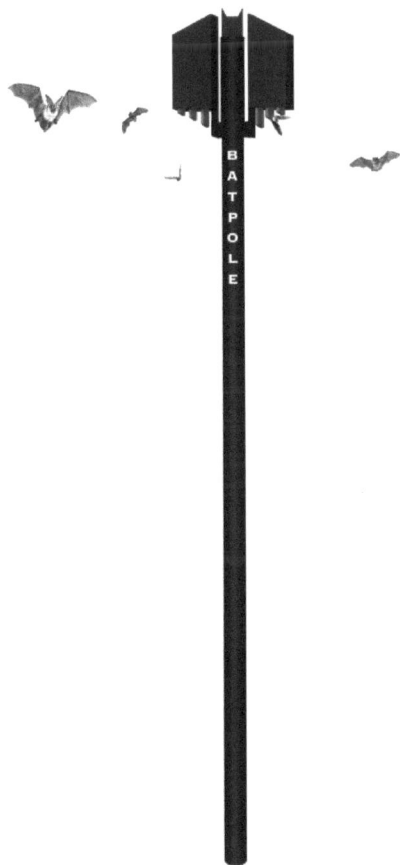

Culture Urbaine
Cloud Collective
Geneva, Switzerland

Algae are exceptional natural machines. Microalgae absorbs CO_2 from urban atmospheres ten times more effectively than large trees.

Microalgae can be used in a range of consumer products, cultivated to produce biofuel, and is naturally rich in essential nutrients such as minerals and vegetable proteins. Research has shown it to be one of the most sustainable long-term sources of biomass able to meet a range of future needs.

The design group Cloud Collective developed a system for algae to grow and thrive in plant-hostile urban environments, such as motorway overpasses.

Culture Urbaine is an algae-growing system installed on an overpass in Geneva, Switzerland.

Its system of transparent tubes, pumps, and solar panels is attached to the concrete siding of the highway overpass. The algae consume the CO_2 created by passing cars and expels clean oxygen. The ample sunlight and CO_2 create ideal conditions for algae to thrive.

The location of the growing unit is an intentional statement "to prove that even these locations of highways and car dealers—despite their anonymous and generic character—can play an important role in the production of food and biomass," says the group.

Eco-Link@BKE, Bukit Timah Expressway, Singapore

Crab Crossing, Christmas Island, Australia

B464 motorway, Böblingen, Germany

ARC Wildlife Crossing, Balmori Associates

Wildlife Crossings

Scientific American estimates that approximately two million animals are killed in collisions with vehicles each year—a number that increases annually and excludes roadkill incidents that don't result in an insurance claim.

A report presented to the Federal Highway Administration noted that "wildlife crossings" in the form of highway overpasses and underpasses "are proven to reduce wildlife-vehicle collisions by an average of 87 percent." The effectiveness of wildlife crossings is being increasingly recognized with a number of them being built to counter the impact motorways have on habitat, species populations, and the disruption of migration routes.

The *ARC: International Wildlife Crossing Infrastructure Design Competition* sought to draw attention to the benefits of wildlife crossings. The competition reported that when the increasing migration ranges wildlife are traveling due to climate change are combined with the fatality rate of animals on highways, "The continents' road systems pose a significant threat to the long-term health and viability of North American wildlife populations."

ARC Wildlife Crossing
Balmori Associates
Denver, CO, USA

The winner of the competition, Balmori Associates, designed a modular crossing system that "utilizes the surrounding landscape in order to create a new shape inspired by nature."

"The design uses a low-tech system of layering wood planes to create an easily modifiable shape. The wood for this system suggests the utilization of local trees felled or weakened by disease."

Originally designed for Vail, Colorado, the bridge isn't tied specifically to the area. "It is a kit of parts," says the firm, "that can be applied and adapted to various conditions and sites."

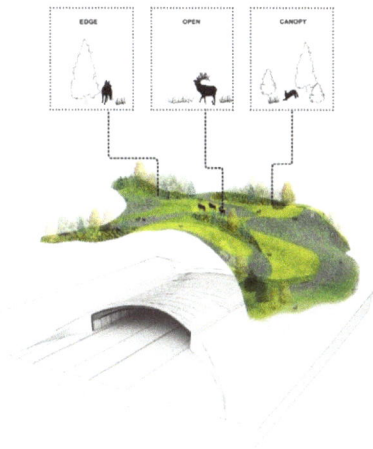

Modular Artificial Reef Structure (MARS)
Reef Design Lab
Melbourne, Australia

"Coral reefs are some of the most bio-diverse and uniquely fragile ecosystems on the planet," explains Reef Design Lab, "and are consequently suffering most drastically and quickly from human expansion."

Modular Artificial Reef Structure (MARS) is a system designed by Reef Design Lab industrial designer Alex Goad. MARS is a complex ceramic lattice that allows for coral frags to be transplanted to its surface and grow to establish a reef ecosystem.

The modular system works like a large underwater Lego set, able to be constructed by divers in a myriad of ways depending on the needs of the site to help mitigate the damage human activity has done to reef ecosystems.

"When a reef system is damaged it can take decades for corals to re-grow to their previous heights, but with the help of an artificial reef, this process can be sped up," explains Reef Design Lab.

"Many artificial reefs do not provide adequate material and surface design to encourage the natural colonization of organisms, leaving the reefs devoid of corals, sponges, and seaweeds. MARS reinvents the artificial reef as a modular system that can be easily manufactured, easily implemented, and tailor made for a majority of applications."

MARS has been implemented on Summer Island in the Maldives where there is a large coral frag farm but no nearby natural reef structures. It was voted one of the top ten inventions of 2015 by Popular Science magazine, and was the winner of the Dyson Australia Innovation Award.

July 2011

July 2012

October 2013

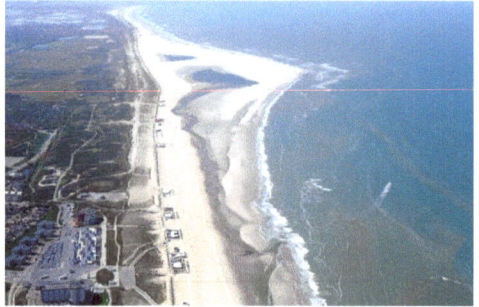

May 2015

August 2016

Delfland Sand Engine
Deltares
South Holland, the Netherlands

Coastal erosion is a problem that gets bigger as our coastlines get smaller. The problem isn't new, and neither is the way it is usually addressed. Often a seawall is built against an eroding coastline, or dump truck loads of sand are deposited to fill in specific spots.

What has been overlooked so far is how the same wind, waves, and currents that caused the erosion might be used to solve the problem. The Delfland Sand Engine does just that.

The Delfland Sand Engine is a coastal replenishment experiment that uses the ocean's natural forces as a tool to repair coastal restoration. Engineers studied tide and wind patterns along the coast of the Delfland region of the Netherlands and installed a 21.5 million cubic-meter repository of sand at a strategic location.

Over the course of several years, "the sand is gradually redistributed by natural processes over the shore face, beach, and dunes," the project reports. "By making use of natural processes to redistribute the sand, this innovative approach aims to limit the disturbance of local ecosystems, while also providing new areas for nature and more types of recreation."

In the parlance of coastal restoration, filling in erosion points with dump trucks of sand is known as "periodic small-scale nourishments," a practice that is not the most efficient nor environmentally friendly method of coastal maintenance.

"An alternative to these periodic nourishments," the project states, "is a mega-nourishment applied every 15 to 30 years. The main advantage of a mega-nourishment over periodic smaller-scale nourishment is less ecosystem disturbance. Moreover, the unit price of the large amount of sand is likely to be less than that of smaller amounts at a time, and nature does most of the distribution work."

BESE-elements
Bureau Waardenburg
Culemborg, the Netherlands

Sea levels are rising and the intensity of tidal waves are increasing—a combination of factors that have a devastating impact on estuary habitats and waterfront ecosystems. Near-shore habitats are also being depleted as increased undertows and dredging make it difficult for species of plants and mussels to anchor themselves and establish a foundation.

BESE-elements is a biodegradable structure that literally provides a foundation for habitat restoration for seagrass, mangroves, and other aquatic species. The units are designed for modular assembly and installation, enabling various combinations of structure depths and dimensions depending on need.

"BESE-elements present a temporary structure and protection for organisms to start growing," describes Bureau Waardenburg.

"After a certain time, sufficient adult organisms have grown and built up a structure on their own for younger ones to settle on. During this process the BESE-elements break down and the organisms establish and enlarge their own structure."

Made from potato starch, the company says that in contrast to many other bio-plastics, BESE-elements "undergoes complete breakdown without the need for composting agents."

"The potential uses for this starch-based three-dimensional structure are almost endless. We are just starting to uncover the possibilities of the diverse range of applications, which include ecosystem restoration, coastal and bank-side protection, water purification, sewage treatment, habitat creation, and aquaculture."

Oyster Reef Balls

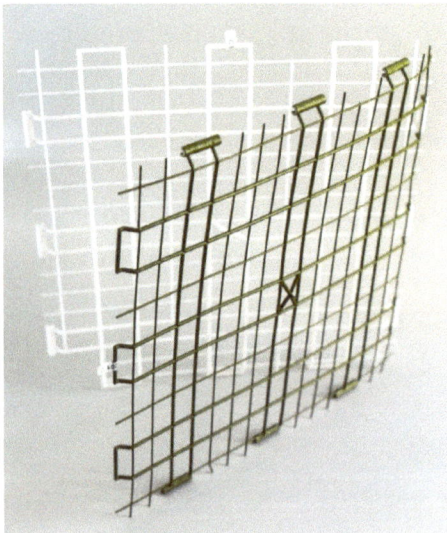

BESE-Gabion

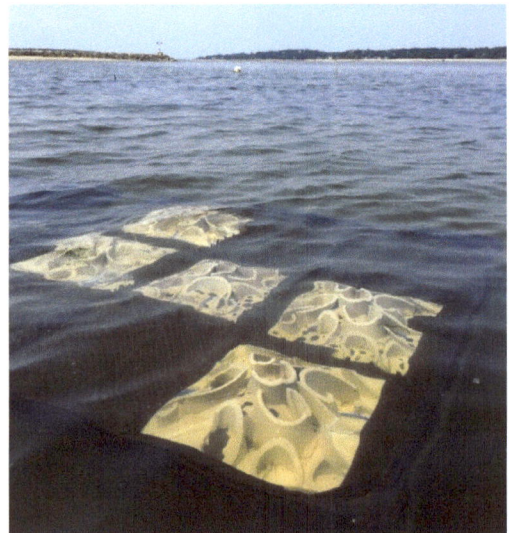

Protoreef

Oyster Restoration

Oysters can filter up to 50 gallons of water per oyster, per day. They are capable of cleaning 80 percent of contaminants from their surroundings in 72 hours, and provide habitat for dozens of other species. Yet 85 percent of the world's oyster reefs have disappeared because of overfishing, habitat degradation, and climate change. Fortunately, there are numerous efforts underway to restore oyster populations with various designs and systems.

Oyster Reef Balls

The Reef Ball is something of a Swiss Army knife for aquatic ecosystems: restoring Mangrove forests in Asia, creating coastal breakwaters in Texas, and replenishing oysters in Nantucket. Its utility is due to a simple, efficient design. Its weight and domed shape prevent it from being toppled by currents, while its holes and texture allows water to pass through the structure and nutrients to cycle over the entire surface of the reef.

CORRD / CORRT

Grow Oyster Reefs (GROW) has designed Concrete Oyster Reef Disks (CORRD), Reef Restoration Tiles (CORRT), and CaC03 Concrete Mix, to enable groups or individuals to contribute to the restoration and enhancement of marine ecology by converting crevices and smaller seawater areas into oyster habitats with modular, affordable units.

BESE-Gabion

Oyster restoration efforts usually use metal gabions to restore oyster reefs. The gabions are filled with oyster shells and placed into the water to recruit oysters, but the metal will rust and pollute the ecosystem. BESE-gabion is made from starch and is fully biodegradable. After oysters have colonized the structure the gabion will fall apart, leaving only the restored reef behind.

Protoreef

Blue W Labs in Wellfleet, MA, has developed the Protoreef, a 3D-printed "biogenic reef restoration structure" to aid in the recovery of oyster populations. Protoreefs are "modular, plastic-free and biogenic," says the company. "They are living, growing, and reproducing with a complex three-dimensional structure for juvenile oyster settlement and protection. Protoreefs can be used to jump-start restoration efforts by creating nodes of biogenic architecture that attract reef-dwelling biodiversity."

Project Smartroof 2.0
Amsterdam, the Netherlands

Green roofs have taken root in the collective consciousness of cities as good and environmentally friendly things.

The Dutch have, as usual, taken a good thing and designed an even better one. Their version is the "Blue-Green" roof system that maximizes the combination of Blue (rainwater catchment, storage, and reuse) and Green (biodiverse) roofs for resilient and climate adaptive cities.

Coined Project Smartroof 2.0, the systems has been installed on the roof of Building 002 in Amsterdam's former Navy Yard.

The new system "captures and stores rainwater in the 85 mm drainage layer underneath the soil. The lightweight recycled plastic drainage units are fitted with integrated fiber technology enabling capillary transport from storage to soil to naturally irrigate the myriad of plants species without the use of pumps, hoses, valves, or energy."

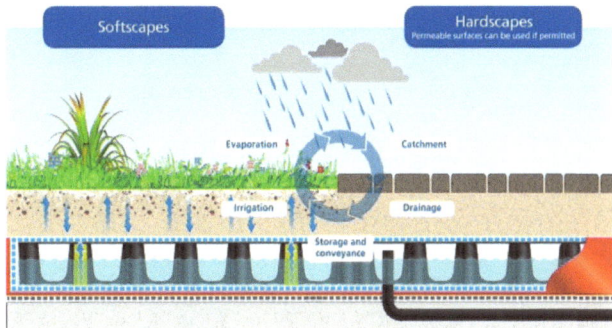

The project is the result of a consortium of public and private partners and knowledge institutes. "The partners and institutes worked together with an open approach to develop the smart roof innovation," describes City of Amsterdam's Sacha Stolp of the consortium. "This was crucial in this project, and I believe an example of best practices in how we can solve the urban issues our cities are facing."

"With Blue-Green infrastructures, paved surfaces such as rooftops and podium decks are transformed into growing green oases, which cool the environment by means of reflecting sunlight and evaporating water. These oases keep rainwater out of the sewer systems, offer a pleasant place to stay for humans, add biodiversity, and reduce the HVAC load of the building underneath."

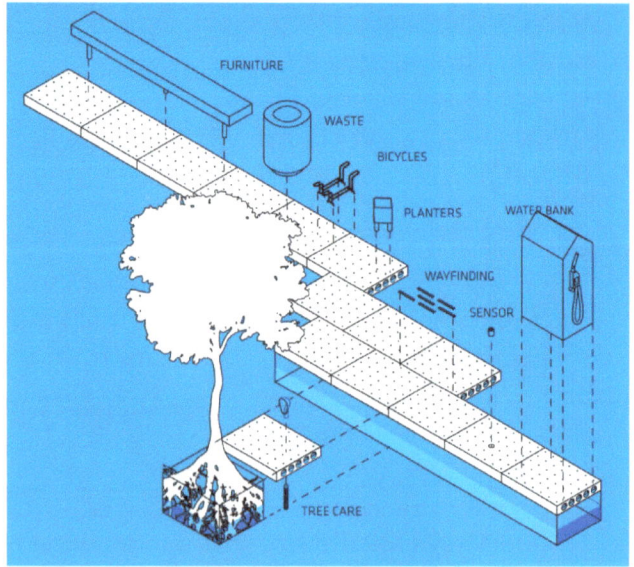

FURNITURE

WASTE

BICYCLES

PLANTERS

WATER BANK

WAYFINDING

SENSOR

TREE CARE

Climate Tile
Third Nature
Copenhagen, Denmark

Third Nature wants to enlist the surfaces of the city in the effort to reduce the impact of climate change.

The firm has developed a tile that enables sidewalks and urban spaces to handle increasing rainfall. The tiles can channel 30 percent of rain away from the city's infrastructure to prevent overloading storm water systems.

"Climate Tile is a modular system that allows water to run down into an integrated underground water-handling system," explains the firm.

"The sidewalks retain their fundamental function but will also provide the city a number of new qualities and functions.

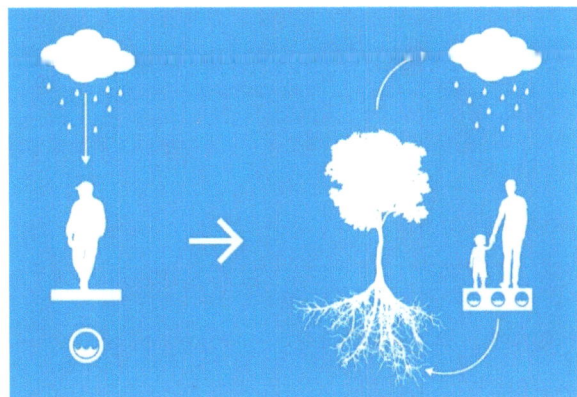

The water management system can connect to a series of urban elements, such as vegetation, water, and playground equipment to motivate activities in the city whilst providing vibrant and natural urban spaces."

"We wish to show the world that climate proofing isn't just hidden technology, but a chance for everybody to participate in the improvement of our everyday spaces where we can understand the city's hidden connections and offer greater quality of life," says Jeppe Ecklon, Project Manager for Third Nature.

"The Climate Tile is a solution that can ease the problems with rainwater that cannot get away, whilst creating more urban nature in our grey streets."

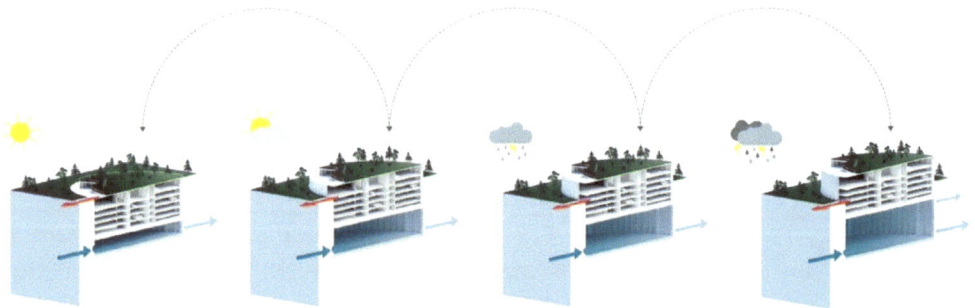

POP-UP
Third Nature
Copenhagen, Denmark

Third Nature has developed their own solution to the urban challenges of flooding, parking, and lack of green space—their POP-UP project addresses all three at once.

"With the quest for green, livable, and human-scale cities, cars and car parking have become an increasing challenge fighting for space in dense cities—often at the price of urban green areas and parks," says the firm.

"At the same time, climate changes force cities to handle huge amounts of storm water generated by more and more powerful cloudbursts, by building large water reservoirs under roads and squares. The situation calls for a rethinking of the way we establish parking, storage of storm water, and new urban spaces."

POP-UP is a structure that stacks a storm water reservoir, parking facility, and urban space into one unit. In the event of heavy rain and cloudbursts, rainwater is led through the sewer's overflow system into a reservoir below the garage. The parking structure then rises up, aided by a system that guarantees the structure remains accessible for cars and pedestrians alike.

The parking system's retaining walls and guide tracks ensure the structure moves steadily and safely when the water level increases and decreases in the reservoir. Once the city's sewage system has the capacity to handle the rainwater, the water is slowly returned to the sewer network, after which the parking structure lowers back into the ground.

"POP-UP will be a temporary but visible player in the cityscape and in a positive way illustrating how our cities can change character and function as the weather changes," says the firm.

CREDITS

Living Seawalls (Fish Apartments)
https://www.reefdesignlab.com/
Image Credits: Reef Design Lab

Living Seawalls (Hex Panels)
https://www.reefdesignlab.com/
Image Credits: Reef Design Lab
Acknowledgements: Sydney Institute of Marine Science (SIMS)

Singapore Seawall Tiles
http://www.science.nus.edu.sg/research-highlights/1793-ecologically-engineering-singapore-s-seawalls
Image Credits: Dr. Lynette H. L. Loke
Acknowledgements: This work was funded by the National Research Foundation, Prime Minister's Office, Singapore, grant number: R-154-000-A26-281 (MSRDP-05).

Floating Ecosystems
https://www.biomatrixwater.com/
Image Credits: Biomatrix Water

Vlotwateringbrug ("Bat Bridge")
https://www.nextarchitects.com/en/projects/vlotwatering_bridge
Credits: Images by Raymond Rutting, NEXT architects; Drawings by NEXT architects

Tern Pontoons
https://www.buwa.nl/en/advice_nature_environment.html
Image Credits: Bureau Waardenburg
Acknowledgements: Tern Pontoons is part of the research program Natural Lake Marker/IJssel (Natuurlijk(er) Markermeer-IJmeer (NMIJ)) of Rijkswaterstaat, done in collaboration with de Vries & van de Wiel, BWZ ingenieurs and Grontmij.

Batpole
https://beecollective.eu/
Image Credits: Bee Collective

Skyhive
https://beecollective.eu/
Image Credits: Bee Collective

Culture Urbaine
https://www.thecloudcollective.org/en
Image Credits: Olivier Arandel / The Cloud Collective

Wildlife Crossings
Eco-Link@BKE; Image Credit: Singapore National Parks
B464 motorway, Böblingen, Germany; Image Credit: Klaus Foehl
Crab Crossing; Image Credit: Christmas Island Tourism Association

ARC Wildlife Crossing
http://www.balmori.com/
Image Credit: Balmori Associates

Modular Artificial Reef Structure (MARS)
https://www.reefdesignlab.com/
Image Credit: Reef Design Lab

Delfland Sand Engine
https://www.deltares.nl/en/
Image Credit: Deltares
Acknowledgements: The Delfland Sand Engine is a partnership between Deltares, Rijkswaterstaat, and the Provincial Authority of South Holland.

BESE elements
https://www.bese-products.com/biodegradable-products/bese-elements/
Image Credits: BESE-elements
Acknowledgements: BESE-elements was developed by Bureau Waardenburg together with Rodenburg Biopolymers and ENEXIO Water Technologies.

Oyster Restoration
Image Credits: The Nantucket Watershed Project www.ackwatershed.org
Grow Oyster Reefs http://www.growoysterreefs.com/; BESE-elements;
Blue W Labs https://www.bluewlabs.com/;

Project Smartroof 2.0
https://en.projectsmartroof.nl/
Image Credits: Project Smartroof 2.0
Acknowledgements: Smart Roof is a Public-Private Partnership between Bureau Marineterrein, Waternet, City of Amsterdam, Drain Products, Permavoid Ltd, KWR Watercycle Research Institute and Aedes Real Estate.

Climate Tile
https://www.tredjenatur.dk/en/portfolio/climatetile/
Image Credits: Third Nature
Acknowledgements: Climate Tile is designed in collaboration with Danish companies IBF and ACO.

POP-UP
https://www.tredjenatur.dk/en/portfolio/pop-up/
Image Credits: Third Nature
Acknowledgements: The project has been developed in cooperation with the engineering companies COWI and RAMBØLL, that contributed to the project with structural models and financial calculations.

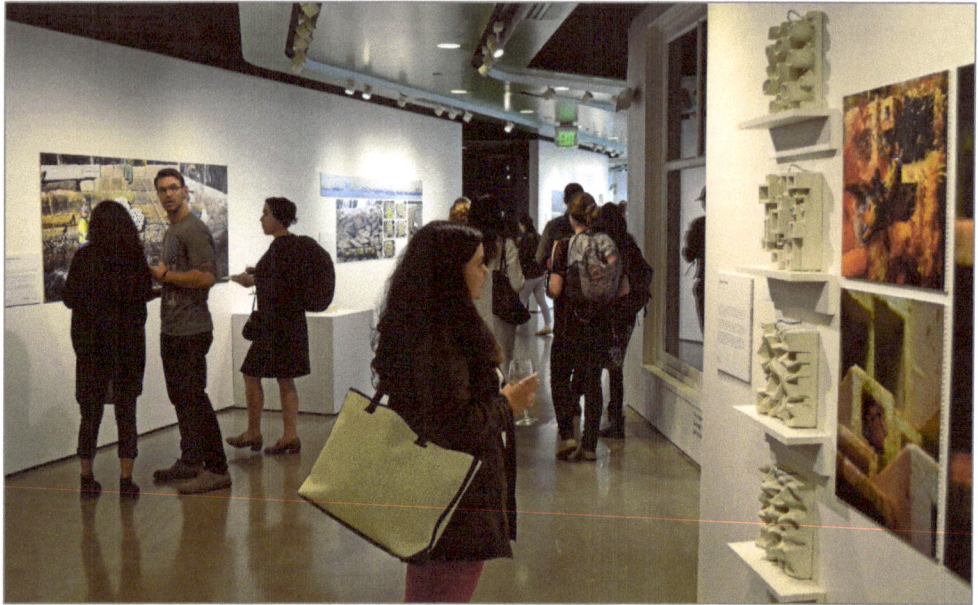

NatureStructure: The Exhibition

NatureStructure is infrastructure designed for nature; work created to nurture and repair ecosystems and habitats and integrate natural processes into the built environment.

The NatureStructure exhibition premiered at the Boston Society of Architects, inspiring a range of new projects to restore and improve its region's ecosystems.

NatureStructure is constantly updated with international projects created to employ natural processes, increase natural environments, and repair ecological damage.

For enquires about the NatureStructure exhibition, contact Scott Burnham at sb@scottburnham.com

www.ingramcontent.com/pod-product-compliance
Lightning Source LLC
Chambersburg PA
CBHW060843270326
41933CB00003B/184